MW00487905

A YEAR *of*

LAST THINGS

A YEAR *of* LAST THINGS

Poems

MICHAEL ONDAATJE

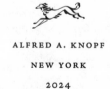

ALFRED A. KNOPF

NEW YORK

2024

THIS IS A BORZOI BOOK PUBLISHED BY
ALFRED A. KNOPF

Copyright © 2024 by Michael Ondaatje

All rights reserved. Published in the United States by Alfred A. Knopf,
a division of Penguin Random House LLC, New York.

www.aaknopf.com

Knopf, Borzoi Books, and the colophon are registered trademarks of
Penguin Random House LLC.

Selected material originally appeared in the following publications:
"5 a.m." in *Brick Magazine*; "Leg Glance" in *London Review of Books*;
"Bruise" and "Definition" in *The New Yorker*; "Evening," "November,"
and "Winchester House" in *Threepenny Review*; "A billiard hall,
cress sandwiches, wallpaper, a piano solo" and "Lock" in *Walrus*.

LIBRARY OF CONGRESS CATALOGING-IN-PUBLICATION DATA
Names: Ondaatje, Michael, [date] author.
Title: A year of last things : poems / Michael Ondaatje.
Other titles: Year of last things (Compilation)
Description: First edition. | New York : Alfred A. Knopf, 2024. |
Identifiers: LCCN 2023024604 | ISBN 9780593801567 (hardcover) |
ISBN 9780593801574 (ebook)
Subjects: LCGFT: Poetry.
Classification: LCC PR9199.3.O5 Y43 2024 |
DDC 813/.54—dc23eng/20230605
LC record available at https://lccn.loc.gov/2023024604

Jacket and case art: *Race at the Uji River* (details) by Soga Shōhaku,
Promised gift of Robert S. and Betsy G. Feinberg, Photography:
John Tsantes and Neil Greentree © Robert Feinberg, TL42147.30
Jacket design by Abby Weintraub

Manufactured in Canada
First Edition

for Linda

and for Zbyszek Solecki

Writing isn't just telling stories. . . . It's telling everything all at once.

—MARGUERITE DURAS

. . . he watched all his characters hiding in his youth.

CONTENTS

A YEAR *of*

LAST THINGS

LOCK

Reading the lines he loves
he slips them into a pocket,
wishes to die with his clothes
full of torn-free stanzas
and the telephone numbers
of his children in far cities

As if these were
all we need and want,
not the dog
or silver bowl
not the brag of career
or ownership

Unless they can be used
—a bowl to beg with,
a howl to scent a friend,
as those torn lines remind us
how to recall

until we reach that horizon
and drop, or rise
like a canoe within a lock
to search the other half of the river,

where you might see your friends
as altered by this altitude as you

The fresh summer grass,
the smell of the view—
dark water, August paint

How I loved that lock when I saw it
all those summers ago,
                    when we arrived
out of a storm into its evening light,

and gave a stranger some wine
in a tin cup

Even then I wanted
to slip into the wet dark
rectangle and swim on
barefoot to other depths
where nothing could be seen
that was a further story

DEFINITION

All afternoon I stroll the plotless thirteen hundred
pages of a Sanskrit dictionary
with its verbs for holy obsessions,
the name for an alcove
of coin washers whose fingers glint
all night with dark lead, grains of silver

Here root vowels take
an accent at high altitudes

the way dictionaries
speak over mountains

A single word to portray light
from that distant village
reflected in a cloud,
or your lover's face lit
by the moonlight on a stage

Landscapes nudge the dialect.
In far places travellers know
a faint gesture can mean
desire or scorn,
                              just as
a sliver of a phrase thrown away
hides charms within its grammar

                    —A guru
"someone with a light touch"
derives from that short vowel, alone
and before a single consonant

Wherever you turn
definitions push open a door

The precisely named odour of a man
who is a heart-thief

a word for the highest complication
during a play used also for impregnation

Attributes of character
link themselves to professions
—a metal worker, the river merchant,
the Commissioner of Oaths,
the census taker of birds who
continues the medieval art
of whistling,

those who carry bees on their arm
like a dark flame,

the sullen recluse
who was once the author
of a prayer

This word for a pool before a temple,

or *a n s a*—"the shape of a shoulder blade"
as in the corner of a holy quadrangle

*

     The ancient phrases
give you the coin of escape
—that epithet for those who return
to broken relationships repeatedly
will row you away from confusion

or remain only for remembrance

This is how deep I was lost,
my darling, in a love so narcotic
I possessed unimpaired splendour
having no other want or wish

What was there before
there was the warmth of that word
for your shoulder blade,
or that time before we moved
to a freedom from desire?

5 A.M.

for Stan Dragland and for Kris Coleman

The wilderness of our youth, an empty barn,
dancing with friends into the small hours,
then daylight and the cars swerving away
wordless into the dawn

It arrives all at once tonight,
not as memory, but like a gift
from forgetfulness,
as a desire can wake you

or this poem
based on the accidental change of speed
in a friend's camera into slow motion.
So now I remember
the rest of our shadows
as we danced, all our heartbeats
under the thunder

and I can speak to you the way
we once sang farewells out of our cars
late at night, when those
goodbyes remembered everything

Let us speak about our enormous flaws as told to us
by others—accountants, wives before leaving—
about how we deceived ourselves, even our dogs
by ignoring their concerned pre-walk, tear-stained howls,
though they rested often on our chests
making sounds like old ships.

For there is only, but *always*, a small tunnel of escape
for forgiveness. As with any novel or film you hang
onto "character rights" and where you came from.
There's not much to leave when you're only fifteen, we are told.

My friend's family in Warsaw during the war
was fed and kept alive by a German deserter
who roamed Europe like Odysseus, even
joining them in their escape, pretending to be mute
while they taught him Polish. A dissolved genealogy
let him cross borders and war zones with them,
finding a path through various armies.
He knew already *the great engines of this world
do not run on faithfulness.*

Without a homeland he was for a while
a father to the children.

And later, more than once, needing a passport
he married more than once.

With dialects and port-accented verbs
he could sing in four languages about departure.
He belonged still to himself at fifteen,
waiting for the later years to reach him.

Who had he become? He'd bunked beside Isaiah,
escaped judgement, remained as if impenitent.
He felt comforted only when—as with the dog—
it became difficult to know if accusations
meant damnation or contentment.

LAST THINGS

Dante's busy writing, say, the Fourth Canto,
and anything could happen.
—ADAM ZAGAJEWSKI

1. Work in Progress

The air in the piazza darkens
around Dante Alighieri
stern, high above us
one hand holding a book,
his nose a dagger
in the blackness

Two nights later I dream
Dante's body is a falling animal,
he crawls out of shattered plaster
a blue rough tongue slithering
from his mouth, as if
at the end of the world
there is this lizard
who will walk up
some staircase in the dark,
a finished book in his mouth

2. The Quick

Adjusting her sandal, losing her hair,
the four of us at breakfast. Our storyline
feels almost continuous these years later
as if we are oaks lining the road
of a linear village, or within
a posthumous diary.

Strindberg dying in bed felt his pillow take shape,
heard crickets and birds singing within it.
Everything around him felt alive.
Or Agha Shahid Ali before his death
writing in a ghazal,
"Before the palaver ends, hear the sparrows' songs,
The quick quick quick, O the quick of it all."

3. Below Dante

I had been alone for weeks when we met there,
below Dante. The three of us lounged in a *pensione*,
I was writing a book about a dying man.
Twenty years later, you were in a bed,
on Brunswick Avenue. And I kissed your feet,
Connie, one of my shy farewells.

It was your year of last things,
but you were luminous,
within those final fires.

Earlier, alone in that city, I had dreamed
the statue falling brutal from its noble height,
and the poet crawling through plaster,
so near to where we met
in that piazza those years ago.

Now we gather our days together—
the countless meals, laughter and argument,
four of us at vicious canasta
(those small and essential feints),
margaritas, the dancing, and once
drunk in a car on some island or other,
all those small recalls of this and that
before our walk up a staircase into the dark.

for Connie and Leon Rooke, Florence, Spring 1990
—Toronto, Nuit Blanche, October 2008

DARK GARDEN

What was the month you stepped, barefooted
(a rabbit's cage fallen open on the grass
below your gaze) onto a nail.
A winter month in the tropics. One of your daughters
recently born. This is all I know of the story.

Not your gasp, or the half collapse
whatever that month was, or even the year.

Where was I in the late sixties?
Somewhere in the middle of a book,
a western with distant violence, and
Sallie Chisum stepping barefoot onto a porch
with Billy to pull a splinter out of her heel.

That faraway echo and coincidence.

So I did not hear the gasp, see her stillness,
or her unheld in that dark garden
during the collapse of everything, a marriage,
no ointment in the house, the children

unawakened, unaware
on that December or perhaps April night
when the darkness took *forever* to die.

Where is that unmarked calendar for 1969
when she cleaned her blood off the mat floor.
A single mother in those missed years,
with only the small glimmer of possibility or luck
still years away from us.

A strange awakening thought at 7 a.m.

to erase this life, and desire what I might have known
in photographs of you before we met

where I could have circled you
at a tactful distance, being told only
about your husband

but nothing of the rules you owned
about yourself, how you raised your children,
were in constant argument with Kailua city planners

Or even before, during that slow crawl
of tectonic plates across the Pacific
into the future with us unaware
of each other at some high-school dance,
a drunken party, or the boy
who was invited to your heartbeat
under a kimono
       The *then*.

All that history until we met
in furious chaos when I loved first
your face, then loved how you
had become what you were

How long did all those possibilities sleep
during the years
before this emerging

A NIGHT RADIO STATION IN KOPRIVSHTITSA

for Miroslav Penkov

I.

Crossing the mile-wide ten-mile depth
of the San Andreas Fault and three time zones
to reach you, be in your company
in what feels like some museum of the night.
We stand under a medieval firmament
of bruised clouds, thunder, old chaos,
a spoke of light hovers to articulate
each noble star and I want to rest
my hard, busy, thought-driven head against
your naked neck and inhale everything there,
any hint of desire, catch the surprising gasp.

When you are surrounded with ornaments
of the old world, you need to hear one living vein.

2.

Ottoman rule prohibited the building of churches
higher than a horse and rider,
so deep pits were cut into the earth
to begin new monasteries.
The breaking of rules in this way
made invisible, as they would be
that nameless night, when you touched her,
but she would not touch you.

3.

The candles in the sunlight of this Bulgarian church
flicker sideways to imitate a village dance,
but above in dark murals the devil pisses
into a bowl, witches stir ointments.

There were the 38 Martyrs of Plovdiv
and 19 Female Sinners whose fates
remain unknown. Just as in painting after painting
of the seemingly never completed Last Supper
there's no betrayal or treason, only a busy table
of garlic, onions, local bread, a squid, a fish.

Most stories remain unresolved,
undiscovered, like the breaking of a rule.

The secret of a famous poet's glass eye
revealed only when found beside
his body in a mass grave near Sofia.

4.

HOW TO PAINT AN ICON

If there is only one eye, ignore the other.
Remove dogs from the upper portions,
they exist only in lower zones, licking the sores
on a beggar or the feet of a returned prodigal.

Depict new rain whenever it arrives over the hills.
No sunlight. Everything is sunlight.

Country eggs in tempera to depict warriors.
City eggs to glisten the serene pale
faces of women in court,
or the imprisoned. Or a saint.

5.

In my notebooks I have written of the silence in icons. As well as of the two great rivers painted onto arched windows in earlier times—the blue of the Tigris and Euphrates—remembered by linen masters journeying to work in Edirne or Thessalonica when there was not enough sunlight to work during each winter in their own villages.

There's always been this deafness in icons. You rely only on gestures from the hierarchy you find yourself within while what appears beyond those painted windows remains silent. You hear no rush of water, or the buckling of clouds. The world outside is icon-less. A metal arm that heals a damaged Madonna is constructed by blacksmiths, not faith. A mother searching for food during famines, who moves from village to village as if from mural to mural, finds only faces turning away. Her son enters a market of artisans to locate the one person to cut down a hazardous thorn tree that contains the madness of his father.

Icons do not travel. They are visited only by the wise during Annunciations. While the Christ child is bathed in a basin, they ignore the far hills where the weather more closely resembles illegal or uncertain histories—a monsoon that once may have travelled a thousand miles, its swirling air plucking every leaf from a forest as it journeyed in some apocryphal Asian tale to eliminate the war at Troy by disguising the location of all those night stars in order to confuse the ships that approached the doomed city. So later there is no evidence in any archive of that historical war. The world beyond icons always remains artless with unpainted lightning, broken coasts.

I tell you all of this quickly for now the hour darkens and a bishop walks through his town towards a home-made fire.

6.

Egg tempera on pine or poplar, or beech,
the Russian variant. Orthodoxy moved
to Moscow—The Third Rome—in 1453.

All lines of focus in the architecture of an icon
meet at the spectator.

Holy faces are rarely in profile.
Judas is always turning away.

*

Though even icons' lives can be unpredictable. They will
now and then need to journey into specific villages to be
repainted—to revive their black eyes with a burned pine
resin or Egyptian blue. While their figures also need re-
construction, despite being static for centuries. These travels
are usually attempted during a peace treaty between wars or
near the end of a dynasty. Rejuvenation assures icons of their
familiarity—the precise measurement of a narrow arm that
holds a Christ child, the aging skin of an advisory saint. Even
that complex swerve in the shoulder of Judas turning away.

Those month-long journeys from Athens, to Sofia, to
Koprivshtitsa, to Plovdiv and beyond, allow them to witness
local history as they travel the rutted roads, as if they too are
moving now within murals of altering despair, poverty, dis-
organized lives, while transported by cart and later by salt-

merchants on ships that eventually tether themselves and their sacred cargo at ports along the Black Sea, where they will remain for a season being rebuilt within the safety and assurance of carefully recorded sea levels.

*

One night in the village of Koprivshtitsa, where Miro and his father and I paused for a night on our journey east, we entered a barely lit dining room in a local inn, where the dial of the small radio lit up its various stations like a miniature firmament. We could hear what sounded like tentative confessions in varying languages.

When Miro and his father went up to their rooms, I remained behind. Sometimes I would recognize a refrain or line from a poem. But most of what I heard was perhaps being attempted for the first time and sounded embarrassed. "Every time I saw you," a man was saying, "I was crazy about you. Even the time you came up to me in that bar and asked me to dance as the jukebox played 'Wild Horses,' and I said no, even then I was crazy about you." A few minutes later a female voice—"Sometimes you don't want to love the person you love / you turn your face away from that face whose eyes lips might make you give up anger. . . ." The radio host gathered these calls from numerous cities without judgement. As if we all were, as a writer once said, "anonymous among thousands, waiting in the dark at great stations on the edge of countries."

I crouched by the black cube broadcasting those excuses that once had rejected someone's desire. Perhaps it was a too carefully protected relationship in that person who now realized it had become with time an untruthful permanence. Perhaps the object of desire had feared the possibility of a capsizing life; but now a refusal felt worse than unfaithfulness, worse than trespass. The confessing voices continued to be broadcast into Koprivshtitsa by this radio station, as if their only intent was to reach just one person who might now perhaps whisper back to them through the dark and alter a previously scared response—on a night when he had touched her, but she would not touch him.

Brighton girls are like the moon, a rough male voice was singing, as that evening of voices began gradually to be replaced by music.

Now and then I hear confessions like these in my own life. I have often listened to a friend who felt self-damned. And once there were three women I sat next to in a bar all evening in Heisler, Alberta, who complained of a mutual friend they had once been obsessed with, eventually singing *he was the first to entice me when I was young* again and again until the words became a chanting when removed from their melody, making it stark judgement, a curse.

I was aware of all this in the darkness of that room in Bulgaria while outside the traffic of carts was transporting delicate objects wrapped in heavy cloth. The atmosphere was of some earlier decade. When the radio's volume began to fade I pressed myself closer against the speaker to hear of someone who touched a woman's neck so she had drawn back awkwardly, who might instead have paused and then returned to him slowly so he could feel her heartbeat at his shirt. But now they both were in this much later time, moths banging their bodies against any available light.

*

Somewhere, while travelling down along the west coast of California, I was shown a photograph of three poets standing together, each half blind, so they had only the perspective and depth-of-field of three eyes among them. One owned a past with the wrong measure of dynamite, another a leaping too-friendly dog, the third a mistaken medicine. They were looking out from their portrait with a strange assurance, ignoring the wounds that limited their knowledge to just a world and a half. It was a gaze without any shyness, with no evident bridge to a further room in themselves. The three well-known half-blind poets with that necessary little bit of poison of ambition seemed not unlike the 38 Martyrs of Plovdiv, or those 19 Female Sinners who stare out from frescoes in another town.

That night in Koprivshtitsa we were billeted in small rooms. We retired early, needing to reach the Black Sea coast by noon. But I was unable to sleep and that photograph of the three poets kept appearing. Each of them had written great poems about love that were complex, lyrical, even with the limited vision of a glass eye, even with the bit of poison in them. I knew two of them well. The third I admired and had once heard read years earlier in a crowded gallery in Europe. I even remembered what their voices sounded like.

Until I began hearing another voice in the dark. "Maybe we had the wrong conversations on our lips," she was saying. And I replied into the dark—"Yes. Or perhaps we had known each other too briefly. There was too much evidence of the past in me. And even the present was still fully in my life."

"I just felt I was holding in my palm this gift," she answered. "A blue-throated barbet—that could have flown into your heart."

"I recall what you were wearing, even now," I answered. "It was that green cotton dress you said later you only wore in airports, that I might perhaps never see again. And I remember when *exactly* it took place. It was the day after I had slept in the thin, uncomfortable bed of Heinrich Heine in Düsseldorf, when I did not even know of you, had not yet even desired you, and was awake all night."

Thuringite, zircon, arkose,
terra rosa limestone. Peat
in the Muthurajawela swamp.

Green marble and rare graphite
in their silent darkness.

On sparser maps the few hidden bodies of water.

On the three floors of the zoological museum
at Marcus Fernando Mawatha
mammals evolving through time,

stilled dioramas of wading birds
stalking the river basins,

with illustrations and weak recordings
of how tailorbirds, hill mynahs,
bill-clatterers, the drongo
alter their plumage and calls
when migrating north.

Night paths of vampire bats,
unable to see in daylight.

Forests destroyed by leaf-cutter ants,

recordings of altitude and dialect,
contour maps of drought,
                    the sound levels
of recorded thunder.

All data avoids the naming of cities,
rivers, ancient harbours.

There is no evidence of human life
save the rarely visited village
of Maha Illuppallama
whose every hour of rainfall
was for some reason recorded
each day in 1931.

Only at the Nadesan Centre
are there dated political maps
with named mass graves,
the thousand illegal burials.

All that is left here on a baked afternoon
is a painted basket, a painted cricket

The pools of Oplontis gone
along with its vast kitchen
The pipes in the walls like dry veins

Only insignificant things survived
the Vesuvian lava and ash

along with names of one or two craftsmen
who conceived a floor design,
a theatre wall, or this desire
in a woman's back so beautiful
you are held there in sunlight,
the brown of her neck's shadow
upon her own shoulder, then falling
onto her still-unrestored lover
without a hand to reach for her

All day the quiet beauty of these
lost things by someone
who was good at women
or figs or perspective
on a table's architecture
before a garden

Nothing else lasted,
as if these might be the only memory
of ourselves when we are gone

Science and patience excavate with brushstrokes
and a house emerges without masters or slaves

Even then there were men and women
like bad swans coaxing you into deep water
or a bed of grass, your lover in your arms,
that basket of figs. All these fragments
wrested away from lava
to remember the end of a world,
how it all had been

when what they had captured, assembled well,
gave them their name

The Panther Artist, The Master of Loss

Those solitaries who travelled through hill towns,
arrived at a rich house and painted a face
responsive to love, froze the look
driven mad by a swan

poured mosaics onto a low table,
gathering the colours of flesh
from joy to helplessness
to clarify the conviviality of death
—that reminder at every building's entrance

One travels into the suburb of Oplontis,
that new villa south of Naples,
is brought in, fed with the servants,
and lauded by them for his famousness

He has recorded the gestures of actors,
evoked the brief want between
man and woman, man and man,
disguising his own name within a corner,

draws the panther, paints a cricket,
then on his hands and knees
makes that skeleton in the atrium
of every household before he leaves

The dangers of the subjunctive mood
when love affairs are still all coal and smoke

and gestures focus on almost stationary details,
a thistle, the moon, an unexpected thrush

In the basic architecture of cricket (apart
from its medieval tone) is the almost sultry
skill of the leg glance that involves
"a very short parlay with the head,"
as Ranjitsinhji said, misquoting Jane Austen

and not bothering to move
from the path of the dangerous ball

It is how you make a song
out of someone else's rumour
far beyond the boundary

having reached for what is remote,
covert during a tender alliance
like hidden stairs down into a pond

Almost sinless, with no moral or latitude
as at the outskirts of a particular kind of writing

I remember the afternoon I kept losing you
at the Evolution exhibit in Cambridge.
It was as if you and I no longer recalled
the small book once central to our lives
that guided us out of aimlessness.

So one of us became the forsaken lover
who someday might wave from a subtitled dream
revealing only a location and time.

How did we let slip each other's hand
in the Carboniferous era on the third floor
before we wandered down towards Triassic times.

In the medieval darkness of the Holland Tunnel
in luminous green paint, on whitewashed walls,
or with thick-fingered writing
on dust in a dry Casablanca aquarium—

> *When last*
> *I held you in my arms, my love, the West*
> *African black rhinoceros was still magnificent*
> *and still alive . . .*

What did you do to Paul Vermeersch?
He has searched for you encyclopedically
in Albacete, in Zagora, in towns
whose names have since changed,
and the maps he relies on have worn out.
In what disguise did you leave him
so that he will not recognize your gait
anymore, or your stare from some famous diorama?

Hunt and Torment. Call but no Response.
In the end words of love reveal just yourself.
Not why, or the wished-for thing.
Only those drivers deep in a tunnel into New York
nod wisely and agree with him.
But it is the black rhino whose loss they mourn,
not the person he once held in his arms.

When it is over it is over,
they say into the passing dark.
There are no longer great nostrils
to scent out the source of torment.
It is a generation since our love,
to justify anger, had a horn, a tusk.

In earlier centuries we were guided
by few travel maps for the heart.

In the east pale lands leading to faith and sacrifice,
to the south rivers of indulgence, forests of caprice,

moral dangers beyond belief.

On illegal afternoons, you avoided wide avenues
to enter la Rue de l'Obscurité, your hesitations
a cloud covering your heart.

The Emperor Babur, bashful during his first marriage,
complained of The Great Impermanence,
and rode through landscapes
"with a hundred disgusts and repulsions,"

there was *perfidie, tendresse,*
whirlwinds in the desert.
He supervised Gardens of Fidelity
with a thousand stonemasons
but what they built has disappeared.

A DISAPPEARANCE

The hand erasing writes the real thing.
—HENRI COLE

The disappearance within a painting of a woman
on a swing under a mango tree

altered by the artist to disguise her identity
just two villages away
                              or perhaps
their change of heart

possibly even the newer alternatives of ink

Now there is only a tree, its branches,
not even the colour of her arms

where she floats in her own gale of stillness,
just ink, watercolour, opaque paper

Kangra, India 1850

RIVER

A river mist in July

no longer the water striders
hurtling downstream

Here we walk the borders of our youth
and gather like insects to firelight—my nephew,
his girlfriend, the dearest intimates

though there were times when my retreats
were currents to avoid

when weather reflected me,
a blue sky with swaying trees
preparing for storm

or the depth of a cloud
under this river, angry at something

There would be hours of portage
upriver, till a lock opened

finally, into August desire

How many hours were we
wind swept? Rain swept?

How long did the dog bark
continually into the night?

I was on a bus for six hours to Fez in those early years
in almost silent conversation with a woman
who had often talked me out of things—a change in life,
a foolishness. And as we spoke the bus travelled
from afternoon to midnight, the desert turning cold,
till I was alone, hungry. I must have imagined her
to have someone to talk with.

We roamed through those brief years of friendship,
pausing at the times we both remembered, her quiet
hand on my sleeve warning me of a flame, her laugh
across the room at something foolish I was saying.
Or once, after her awkward confession of a betrayal,
acknowledging *"It was the sixties!"*—a time when I
was still naïve, unaware of the secret lives in others.

We approached Fez, our recollections unfinished,
startled by the lateness, our imagined dialogues a dream.
Earlier she'd murmured how gentleness implied suffering.
Who said that, I asked. "Oh, a woman, of course,
involved with one man most of her life."

And my long-ago friend on that swerving night bus
recited into the dark—

"I don't want to confuse the world anymore with songs about love."

They sound like the giant creakings of a wooden ship
that never comes into port these days . . ."

I said nothing. I knew the two of us loved privacy,
had never shared the solitude within ourselves.

"She has a great poem about Eurydice," she whispered,
 "fearing a man's public light, fearing to be brought home,"
as if this were the essential clue to all stories.

A gust of rain entered the windows of our bus
travelling from Marrakesh to Fez. The darkness hiding
us from others. I was imagining journeys
we might have taken during some pause in her life,
or mine, to a city as unknown as we were to each other
with nothing or perhaps everything between us.
"Yeah, that would have been nice, to travel alongside you,
sometime," saying this in a thoughtful exaggerated drawl,
inventing the voice to defend the secret in herself.
"We could have discovered each other wildly, somewhere,
in Carthage, in a strange room, our bed on its rollers
shuddering on bare wood until it hit the wall, with us
hardly knowing where or even who we were."

She had never spoken that way to me, but in those
never-given-to-us hours beside strangers, truth
needed to be nothing more than a whisper,
the way the wet skin of her shoulder felt private
against mine, damp from the earlier rain.

"Tell me, will you," she was saying, thoughtfully,
"after all these years, tell me what you think of me."
Then looking down at my wanting hand—*Really.*

A narrow lane with dentists crouching in sunlight,
lady barbers, book repairers, sarong tailors.
Along the post office wall a gathering of mynahs
in their youth being trained to sing, the way
you transmit knowledge to a descendant.
Sea Street and Moon Street. Along Hulftsdorp Street,
at pavement level beside the Supreme Court,
a quicker solution to legal cases during a divorce,
as if simply re-threading metal ribs of umbrellas
after a storm.

Elsewhere meetings on the art of praise, the slow skill of forgery.
Street scribes who clarify the few rules of marital love,
then swerve to articulate a sudden desire.
Tragedy, they say, is impossible where Fate depends
on incomprehensible knowledge.

At midnight the stern entrance of dyers who steal colour
out of the bark of trees to paint temples.

Wounded by experience, his exits
barred by repetition, the pianist
cannot escape the rondeau

A dancer in bouts of shyness
refuses to leave the dark

The poet in Haifa does not wish for another word,
knows every newspaper in America seems against him

In St. Jacob, the best musician I know
teaches old people in a nursing home to sing

The foot of the cellist as she played tonight,
off the beat, testing herself in public

The fingers of the telegraph operator in Fonseka
mute, at ease in radio silence
                                    as shyness will
in certain writers thrive in the pages of a book

The high-wire artist, Abdallah Bentaga,
content for now in a famous convict's arms

What safety does anyone own
but the inescapable rondeau

Scholar masters of Japan, once samurai,
lived recluse, almost unreadable
in their compassionate gaze

They built isolated huts
with old war blades
and memories of distant battles—
those wounds like sleeve openings
that left unspoken shadows

It was the era of poets
as still undiscovered pathways,
not a song-maker among them

They would plot a garden with seeds
gathered during travels,
their first broadcast flung into the dark

then listened within that unlit hut
to what hovered out there

All night a samurai alertness,
the stillness learned
as a boy from an owl,
holding the pulse of that garden
in his ink brush, to bring
what was there onto the page

*

It was a time when the subject of poems was love
when not in love, with women collaged out of the past
and recalled in a four-line gaze,
a song without shadows, as if
they had sauntered into life
for only a moment,
                    to be sketched
—a woman walking to the right
while glancing slyly left

the way a forester's child might stumble on
and remember just one
melody of cicadas,
or a poet hurriedly retire a verse with
                    pitch black / sumac

They were busy with memory,
chanting poems while ill, making fun
of the nightingale, listening to
a night rain worrying the flowers,

or that bell in a Zen temple
"sung by pine and cedar"

Elsewhere a crowded age, prodigal with gossip
against solitary writers—like that one-armed poet
drowned in the river with a lightning bug
clutched in his grasp,

                    or those Drunken Immortals
portrayed in the style of "the trembling brush"

But there was also now and then
a walk into a masterpiece
of accident—a nun composing

   The well rope has been
   captured by morning glories—
   I will borrow water

A few syllables from the past

"Some things I just covet," my friend says
when I show this to her
three hundred years later

For years I wrote during the day
above a veterinarian

The howls, the heavy breathing, the sighs
from that faraway untranslated world

The youth in his mask, his hand reaching
off camera as if towards a river,
what did he wish for then?
Almost anonymous, half made, yet that hand flung out
towards some want or discovery,
with so much still to yearn for.

Later someone will charm him
and he will row out to farther depths
following the notes of an unknown bird,
eventually waking in a forest,
asleep against her arm.

Younger he had retreated once from an embrace
and woke later within that desire,
as if it could have been a longer night, an open window.
He remembers it like some unread letter, written long ago.

It was his time without maps.
His only journeys were in books with curious plots,
led by a convict, a railroad saga, or a long-distance love affair
where he'd need always to skirt those ships of Tarshish,
escape the hulks in the marsh country.

Following the hand beyond the camera's reach
in a small café, that partially lived life.
The heart not yet broken or guilty,

everything still under the mask,
the future to be gathered later.
This feather of an unknown bird
left on a desk by a child, or the sketch
of an unfinished blue heart.
But that afternoon, what was his hand reaching for
from the small corner of his world?

TWO PHOTOGRAPHS

It was years earlier, you in an old bathtub
with barely a few inches of water,
on an island, the weather outside unknown
but for the tan that surrounded your whiteness

Everything suggested an era long before the present,
the late sixties perhaps, a weekday afternoon
with little to show how you spent your days, your nights

Just two black-and-white photographs.
The first capturing your gaze into nowhere
the other when you covered your face with your hands
so you were not anonymous, only unseen
except perhaps by what you might be thinking

What was the year? Where was the house and town?
Nothing given away by your silence and careful movement,
"still practically a bride," twenty years before we met

Another photograph I saw later
a more formal nude shaped by shadow
your bare feet, you in a crouch, faceless.
Not so much your image but a husband's
hovering with a camera.

Whereas everything casual in the earlier pictures
with that bathtub and raw sunlight

makes them your ex-husband's masterpiece
—the secret of your look, the recall
of an afternoon when things will hold
or fall away
               It is in these pictures, being
the unknown stranger, I hold
a complete belief in you, long before we met.

How *did* we meet, I whisper even now,
as if magically that first time landing
after a far journey upon a dark
hardly lit island late at night. And then
somehow solitary with you in what
for all I know was a crowded car

from dark rural highways
into a city wild with light
I remember you in a rented car
in blackness, a loose map on your knees
both of us tense with sudden geography

Or in an airport bus after days of solitude
as if returning to this planet from another
with time pushed back into our bodies
only our eyes holding on to each other
with the danger of our love

Books, women, the celebration
of another's talent, a country meal,
a knowledge of birdsong,
who could ever defeat all that in you?

Still, a harassed man,
living always beside
the tear-wet face
with a desire to escape
what he once had loved

A courteous and troublesome animal

There were years he lied like a troubadour
standing near an open door,
                              gathering
what he knew, then going forth
on suburban roads, whistling
to test the range of a woodlark
or bluethroat,
depending on what valley
he entered or what far castle
he travelled to, the maiden indoors
he wants, who thinks
he thinks only of her

He knew earlier generations,
those barons and earls,
born among them, drops their names
into conversations in bars among the roughs,

writes lectures at sea approaching America,
converses with a woman on an ocean liner
through some archipelago
who performs in a women's orchestra

He appears to barely listen. But he listens

He remembers the jade
in the night of her hair,
even if not remembering
for a moment, her name

His was always a life with three courtyards

He could have run away with her,
Ford tells his writer friend, the one
searching now for a plot

What he knows of craft
he never keeps to himself.
He knows water surfaces appear hard
in a Japanese garden. That a rock
in variable light and shadow
is soft as drapery, in the way he is
semi-cursive, leisurely on the surface

It makes women nod "imperceptibly" at him,
they somehow know he can
distract strangers from their nests,
this man on whom no gesture is lost

the great names

Arnaut Daniel, Peire Vidal, Bertran de Born
—restless *jongleurs* of the twelfth century,
the boys of Ventadorn—celebrate
their persuasion of another's charms
—her ankle braced against a wall,
the recognition of the feint

Their craft skillful in elusiveness
could imitate the sound of wood pigeons
as rain showers approached. They composed
as birds sang or in the dialects
of their professions

                    They married widows,
were buried in abbeys.

Years earlier a small creek
across centuries—Lady Murasaki
alone in her hills, the maple leaves scarlet,

"I wish I could show you the colour of my sleeves."

We were the unselected ones, mynahs in our youth,
kept from certain classrooms without knowledge
of what was taught there—the complex sciences,
foreign novels, even rhetoric and courtesy
that might help on some future afternoon
within the corridors of power.

While we were stalled in "The Geography Sixth" studying
flood-plains, maps of far pilgrimages, coastal profiles
of islands drawn by mariners in earlier times.

Still I made my best friends there, in that class
where we talked without pause and with no fear
of boredom. David Gearon, Stuart Blackler,
Geoff Maile, Jeremy Bottle—all my sad captains
raucous beyond midnight
at that wise age of seventeen.

In retrospect we were only discovering ourselves,
immersing ourselves in unnecessary things—
hard-boiled thrillers, how to tap a phone,
the rag-and-bone blues of Radio Luxembourg.
We slipped from school into a dark field,
drank from a bottle, rode a loose horse, and were thrown,
while R B (name withheld) hoisted his Chinese girlfriend,
a composer's only daughter, on a rope

up to his second-floor dormitory, her slipper
floating to earth.

It would be a decade, though it felt just a weekend,
before I stood in front of a Fragonard in the Wallace Collection,
its rapid brushwork of the woman's dress on a swing
reminding me of their quiet whispers as they plotted her ascent,
then noticed that shoe in mid-air, leaving her right foot.
The lighter genius of Fragonard.

It was some time before we were drawn to erotic pleasures
and the disguises of clothing. "A long dove-grey shirt"
on an "idle bride" in a mountaineering thriller, that "air-blue gown"
in a stanza of Hardy, those evolving disguises of the Count
of Monte Cristo, or in the way Stendhal owned 350 pseudonyms
for he disliked the first-person pronoun.

It was now escape from our contained lives that obsessed us
as when Julien in *The Red and the Black* leapt
from a wife's window during an interrupted seduction
into the dark and was chased by friendly guard dogs
who knew him well (that wonderful detail)
"while a husband's bullets whistled past him."
"You close a perfect chapter and it sounds like a gunshot,"
I read in a Polish essay and knew where it came from.

We were witnessing how characters evolved
from a fragment to become assured though
more damaged, revealed but better hidden.
Youth never remains a sentence.

Even if some were pulled by thick ropes
into dormitories, while others, thrown by the horse, lay
drunk on the grass, without hope of a significant life.

And yet with those dutiful maps of pilgrimages had come
the sudden discoveries of un-named islands. Though we still
had no idea whether we might leap up or down
into a further story.

A BILLIARD HALL, CRESS SANDWICHES,
WALLPAPER, A PIANO SOLO

Beckett, they say, read his Bible for style,
Stendhal the Napoleonic Code.

The Ames billiard hall in *The Hustler*
during the first thirty-five minutes. And again
in the final scene.
                    Or a slower duration of time
during the ball in *The Leopard*, and in the memory game
in *Days and Nights in the Forest*.

Picnics by Monet, Titian, the Elder Bruegel, grand lunches
in the Bois de Boulogne with concealed orchestras in a grove,
or Ratty with Mole consuming cold chicken ham pickled gherkins
french rolls cress sandwiches ginger beer, along their river.

The wallpaper in Proust's bedroom, 1882, while he was a boy.

"Les Oignons!" by Sidney Bechet, Paris, 1949, shouted aloud
as everybody danced.

That piano version of "The Man That Got Away" by Bill Charlap
you listened to, solitary at midnight, his slow thoughtful chords
defeating the great damned eloquence of the words

during those hours when we lose interest in what needs to be done.

HIS CHAIR, A NARROW BED,
A MOTEL ROOM, THE FOX

Doubt or unawareness in the self-portraits of artists.

The photograph of Lucian Freud embracing a live fox,
his wrist intimate against the heart of the animal,
not caring how he looks, unmirrored.

The way Robert Creeley and Robert Duncan face you
with the gaze of just one man between them.

Rembrandt's *Self-Portrait in a Feathered Velvet Cap,
with a Proud Bearing.* Then *Self-Portrait with Beggars,*
the *self* pushed aside.

Zhu Yun Ming, who after wild cursive fame retired,
and let his characters dissolve into abstraction.

Those who photograph their shadows on walls
so direct light will not reveal them,
too much knowledge already of the self.

(Degas wished to be illustrious, not well known.)

"See that shadow on the wall," Steve Earle sings,
"doesn't look like me at all . . ."

A watercolour of Goethe at a window
his back to us, my favourite portrait.
Or Gladstone making notes during old age,
all his focus on his pen, as if blind to the world.

During his last performance on stage as *le malade imaginaire*,
Molière, severely ill, was made up to look the picture of health.
They carried him coughing blood from the theatre to his home
(Purcell's music heard as they climb the stairs).
Nuns from a convent surrounded his bed,
as actors playing apothecaries had swarmed
round him on stage an hour earlier.
There was no priest to pronounce absolution.
The now-four-hundred-year-old leather chair he sat on
in the theatre that night used since only by actors in that role.

Strindberg in a narrow bed during his illness
could take no salutes in person. They placed
red lamps by his window so torch-bearing crowds
recognized his balcony. Lear-like, he gave
all his perceptions to the world
—swifts, sparrows, foxes—
"There are times when I hear a cricket sing
in my pillow. It chimes and rhymes
all the remaining night, the way
sounds made by grasshoppers
come from under the surface of the earth."

At the Hacienda Motel in Los Angeles Sam Cooke was shot dead.
"See that shadow on the wall . . ." All those motels and hotels

in literature and song, where X wrote this,
where Y got drunk, where Z overdosed.
The one Hank Williams was driven past, dead already in his car.
The Slavianski Bazaar Hotel in "The Lady with the Dog,"
where Dmitri imagines their dark but hopeful future.
The Hôtel de ville de Courtrai, where Verlaine shot Rimbaud.
The Casa Verdi in Milan, where retired opera singers were welcomed
along with various heteronyms of Fernando Pessoa in their afterlife.

NOVEMBER

Where is my dear sixteen-year-old cat
I wish to carry upstairs in my arms
looking up at me and thinking
be careful, dear human

Sixteen years. How many days since
I found you as if an urchin in a snowstorm

and you moved in assured
learned the territories of the house
and what became your garden

Only now do we see the horizon
where you paused two or three times
then slipped into

Was it too soon or too late
that last summer of your life
when we watched your walk
down to a river to take a sip
from its ongoing flow

Oh Jack I miss your presence everywhere
in the corners of rooms, in every chair,
or nesting in a cardboard box

Take me back where the past can again enter
those early remembered rooms, our snowbound street,
lift me upside down in your arms, I cannot stand it

I need a journey too. Have I slept my life away,
do I understand anything? Will I wear a bell
like yours into the afterlife where language
no longer exists and we gather only linked sounds
like oars from a passing boat,
       those few syllables
to recall tenderness

You no longer wait for us

All day long, Bashō wrote,
A lark sings in the air
Yet he seems to have had
Not quite his fill

1912

When that English novelist returned to poetry
he learned again the breaking line's breath-like leap
into the missed life

till there was no longer a story, only stillness
or falling.
He'd altered so many truths as prose
it was like herding cattle.

How she had silently kissed him
on her night lawn,
then kissed him again.
It was where they had once begun
that other life.

STELLA

This morning before daybreak a thunderstorm

In the last hours before her death
her enemies came. A raccoon, that storm,
the FedEx truck manned by a gentle woman
who'd recently lost her own dog.
Considering the woman who was usually her enemy
our dog perhaps read the grief in her,

just as, the night before, a raccoon
along the fence backlit by moonlight
watched our dog drink noisily from the fountain,
her thin body so thirsty! never sensing
the creature who continued
along the fence and disappeared

So many things to learn, keep on learning
during these last days, watching us
with an awareness that we perhaps
have not learned but shall

Now we are less. How do we become more?

How to die courteous and beautiful
protecting her house, guarding our door

EVENING

That poet you scorned
for retiring when he was forty

then beginning thirty years later
with the same voice and style,
the crack in his life invisible

What he said in youth
and approaching death
having the same breath
that precise pitch
unaffected by time

What a wonder I think now
after all those wars and eras
of love he must have passed through

not one gesture altered
as he wrote, as if he always slept
this way beside her

What could we learn
by leaving the colour blue
for another

There is a film he saw, made over sixty years ago, about a man who travels through time, searching for an image he recalls from his youth. The journey involves an old-fashioned time machine and a romance, although the man's adventure is presented with detachment, like something found in an archive among reels of black-and-white films. Somewhat like early abandoned footage by Robert Frank. A male narrator speaks quietly in French while the camera and subtitles trace their way over photographs that have been collected, until there is shockingly a sudden three-second fragment of movement—as if in violation of the rule that nothing can be seen moving in the past; yet it remains there, almost a dissolve, almost hidden among the hushed, laconic narration and those exhausted black-and-white photographs assembled to depict the narrative plot. It is a film about this man pulling up from the well of his memory an image of the woman he is in search of, who is possibly a compass point from the past.

To make such a journey into the past he goes through the pain of injections and suffers the attachment of a padded helmet to his head that seems to have been cobbled together by amateur scientists in some other era. It is difficult, almost impossible, to reach this woman. Each journey he takes could bypass her or lead to his death. It would be easier to give up this quest. The fact that he speaks with no one in his own world and that he alone has been selected for such journeys of reconnaissance by officials and scientists emphasizes his aloneness and his seemingly passive lack of involvement in his fate. Though he was not a random choice. He was chosen because of that childhood memory he thinks has nothing to do with any talent or any heightened sensitivity that might be found in him.

Seeing the film on video one can be intellectually thrilled by it, but it is only after seeing it on a large screen at, say, a *cinémathèque* that the watcher becomes emotionally linked to it. The science fiction film gradually becomes more self-reflective as it becomes a love story. During one of his journeys the man and the woman visit the Museum of Eternal Animals. She peers at some extinct, dark creature in a glass case—you don't really see it. You see mostly the woman's back, her neck. She is lifting her hair with one hand and you sense she is unaware she is doing this—it may be just a small readjustment to free her hair from her collar. But it is not the woman who is being watched now, any more than it is the creature in the glass case. To the left of the frame is the man's face, fractionally in profile, watching the lifted hair that frees the sight of her neck, revealing its almost sheer nakedness to him. The Egyptians, the viewer remembers, believed the neck was the least protected part of the human body and placed a falcon there, to guard the back of the neck even on their statues.

She is studying an extinct half-seen creature. Just as he, a traveller who has moved back in time, knows he is watching a woman now dead who was once somehow part of his own chronology, for now he is visiting her in her brief present life. She is like one of the eternal animals that surround them. And he is falling in love with her. He could stand there like that for hours, hypnotized by the light bathing her neck.

We have all done this. Once on a plane I was looking at a woman's neck across the aisle three rows ahead of me, and as if in reaction she put her hand up and felt her neck, turned around and saw me, each of us caught in the other's gaze. A moment of balance—before we are tipped in one direction or another.

The film, 28 minutes long, is one of the perfect units in film history. It often feels to me like the first movie ever made, with its almost ridiculous props—an old diving helmet, what looks like a dentist's chair, the old Sebald-like cache of photographs used to reveal the story—and made, it seems, with very little money. It makes you feel as if you are seventeen and this is your first love story.

About thirty years ago a friend from my childhood, Skanda, gave me a photograph of a boarding school in Colombo I had gone to at a very early age for two or three years. Skanda was a relative but only in the Sri Lankan sense where everyone you knew was considered a relative, just as any person who visited members of your family would be referred to as "uncle" or "auntie." What he gave me was a photograph of Winchester House, the junior school in St. Thomas' College. Five years older than I, he had been a boarder there too, and had created an almost heroic reputation as a troublemaker. Even as an adult, I recalled incidents he had been involved in, and later when I became a writer I was tempted to write about his double-edged reputation that mocked any discipline. Then I lost touch with him. He seemed to roam in some far distant territory, with that adventurous nature, yet somehow it felt he would always be a part of my life.

When Skanda and I met for the first time as adults, it was at a crowded dinner in Colombo. We barely spoke to each other. I assumed he was bored with the reputation he still carried of being that notorious troublemaker in his youth. We had come from much the same background and neither of us, I suspect, really wished to go back to that other country of our childhood. When we said a brief goodnight on leaving I did not enquire what he did, and he did not ask what I was doing, though by now I was writing novels.

So far, I had not written about Skanda. At times I might have borrowed an aspect of him that clashed with the safe social world of Colombo, but when I began my novel *Anil's Ghost* Skanda re-entered my world. What I needed was a doctor in one of the peripheral hospitals in the north of Sri Lanka, behind enemy lines during the war. It was a dangerous time. Sometimes the doctors worked throughout the night, then slept half the next day unaware of daylight. I had met such doctors in the north while researching the book. Many had tempers, but were also benign, even compassionate; yet none of them felt themselves trustworthy. I needed a figure with all those aspects. And I needed an outsider, a stranger to the north, who was shocked at what he was now somehow becoming. He "felt happiest when he stepped from disorganized youth into the exhilaration of work," I wrote, having to imagine how that might have happened to Skanda. In any case he now entered my book in a major role, disguised and unexpected, the stranger I needed to build the portrait I was making.

Kurosawa in his autobiography claimed he would always leave the detailed colouring of the central characters in his films up to the leading actors. It was *they* who would provide aspects of their nature he did not fully know. They were the ones who would make those fictional characters vivid, believable. In a similar way I drew on Skanda as well as others I had met—for instance one surgeon who tested his blood pressure at least twice a day when he had a spare moment at a besieged hospital. Or the eye surgeon who did not have the right high level of medical degree for hospitals in the south so was working in the peripheral hospitals at Aralaganwila and Welikanda. The surgical team kept altering her name on medical reports to stop her being dismissed by the authorities. My fictional Skanda, who was a senior surgeon and head of triage, insisted on this. "She's got an unreliable diploma, but she works hard, and I'm not letting her go." Just as he had supported a Cuban there for one year by providing him with a translator. Like the actual doctors I had met, these doctors travelled everywhere, worked anywhere—in abandoned train stations, in clinics housed in partially built schools, in a shaded forest. Skanda became a frame for me by his habit of never feeling wise enough or trustworthy enough, being changeable and inconsistent; gradually emerging within what Penelope Fitzgerald called "the once-born and the twice-born plot which makes a reader (even if he is reading it for the twentieth time) want to interfere at every stage."

This group of doctors realized it was a time that would alter their lives. "They would learn everything of value here. Not one of them returned later into the economically sensible careers of private practice." They woke and walked barefoot, in sarongs, at dawn, onto a narrow country road, half awake, half smiling for no reason in this new yet still ancient universe, as if lords of another time, unsafe, honourable somehow. Now and then Skanda would persuade the eye doctor to recite something, perhaps a story or lines he had heard her say before, her voice always at peace, safe, in the way women are able to hold cats.

Where they found themselves was an apt fit for those with constantly suspect natures, caught now against both sides of a war. They felt safer within their own rules, as Skanda always did, truthful only to himself, even if he felt irrelevant in the world. At night, "they would lie there for a moment locating themselves, trying to remember the shape of their room in the dark. Or they would wake too soon and it was still only three hours past midnight, and they feared they would not go back to sleep again but did so within the sweep of a minute.... They lowered themselves into the bed or cot or onto the rattan mat, on their backs or face-down, usually on their backs because it allowed them the pleasure for a few seconds of resting, with all their senses alive, certain of coming sleep. Someone coughing during the night. The eye nurse in the next bed whispering to herself the way she always whispered to her patients, to make them safe in their darkness. She always rose before the others to read the minimal light as to where they all were." Ampara? Manampitiya?

It was during these pages in the book, when Skanda is among the other doctors, that I could always somehow relax, just remain curious about what was happening, about the dis-coveries of their character. It was strange, for the book was full of biographical and autobiographical intimacies. And yet I was at ease. It was that further intimacy that comes with trusting a fiction, a non-personal truth, going towards what you do not yet know. You will not even remember writing it.

So there would be a character named Skanda in *Anil's Ghost*. But the real Skanda would also appear more fully as another doctor—Gamini, the brother of the book's central male character. And it was Gamini who would claim during his first meeting with Anil that *he* was the black sheep of the family. Gamini still hanging on to an old anarchy of spirit, just as Skanda never saw himself as part of a clan or a fam-ily but as formed by his own nature during his early years at that boarding school in Colombo.

In any case it now felt a coincidence, especially as we did not see much of each other, that when I returned to Sri Lanka as an adult for a family wedding, it would be Skanda—whom I had already imagined into my fiction as a doctor—who, discovering I had also been a student at Winchester House when young, took the trouble to hunt down an old photograph, and then drove over to Battaramulla where I was staying with a friend and, not pausing more than a few minutes, handed it to me as if it was not as innocent as it seemed.

The boys who boarded at Winchester House Junior School ranged in age from seven to nine. Looking at the picture now you are conscious that they were not much older than infants in the old black-and-white photograph intended to capture a moment of childhood innocence. Sixteen students in black shorts and white shirts are playing cricket, while in the background is a one-level building with a tiled roof looking as anonymous as an old cafeteria,

or prison. On the far-left side of that building—it was what I sought out first—was the Housemaster's bedroom, where you were sent to be caned. The rest of the long narrow building was a dormitory, where two rows of twenty beds were separated by a narrow aisle that led ominously to the Housemaster's door.

Out of sight, on the far side of the building, was the kitchen as well as the domicile of the nurse. Also the showers with a minimal and almost medieval toilet. But in the photo we see only the children playing cricket, the bowler having just flung the ball. It's a faraway and anonymous scene that attempts to summarize an average day of childhood. No one is recognizable, but this is the place where Skanda and several others lived and then escaped from after learning a few crucial lessons.

It was the era when official photographs of children were uncommon. No children holding up medals after a swimming event or behaving badly in the background at a wedding. We slipped through youth almost unrecorded, not even able to identify a faint image of ourselves years later. As if we had not been present at all. Although we recalled those lineups for a vaccination or the more feared line waiting to be thrashed by the Housemaster after causing a small riot in the dormitory, or perhaps just laughing too much when the lights went out. So we barely remembered the streets we walked on, or the beds we slept in for years. It was a silenced past and, with its memory of fear and trauma, difficult to step into. Until in my thirties I was handed a black-and-white photograph by a distant hero from that time.

. . .

Some years ago, I read a strange and remarkable poem—now only half remembered—where the speaker in the first line suddenly wakes from sleeping with a woman, rises, leaves the house and ends up in a dark forest fighting his way through the low branches. It felt storm-like, claustrophobic. Eventually after two or three pages he returns, lies down, and the woman asks, "What was wrong?" And he says, after a pause, "An eyelash."

In one of my later books a woman in her twenties confesses to the man she works with, a close friend, about a moment in her past as a teenager which she feels has scarred her for life. She then describes what happened. The man she is speaking to—he was in the Vietnam War and in a benign way tries to calm her and to put all that into perspective—says, "That was just an eyelash." For the listening girl, the phrase releases her from some demon that had overwhelmed her. It felt shocking in its simplicity, and without the context of that original poem by Frank Stanford even more so.

"When you travel you step back from your own days, from the fragmented imperfect linearity of your time," writes Lucia Berlin. "As when reading a novel." And it is also true as you gather distinct fragments you come upon from a remembrance, some of which could belong to another, during the hunt for your own story. As with photographs, the world is deliriously random, inarticulate. You smell sawdust or hay and it reminds you of a summer when you were twelve, or five; even if, as in the story of Jackie Stewart, the Scottish racing car driver, you are at that moment in the midst of a Formula 1 race and in the fierce lead, you suddenly become aware of the smell of hay in the midst of petrol fumes while going 200 miles an hour and encased in noise, the shake of the Ferrari against the wind, the crowd. So that when the race was over he left the victory celebrations and slowly drove the length of the track again several times to try and locate the source of that smell of hay he had passed, which had slipped by him as an echo of a distinct memory of childhood, of being on a farm as a youth, all the while cocooned in fumes until he stopped the car. And saw a few bales of hay on the side of the track at a dangerous curve.

The source of what might become a large plot or an influence on a character may be as small as a glance at a painting or your fear of forgetting your multiplication tables. The influence might even remain that small but still be essential to the person in the story, continuing to alter him or her. A hidden site of pleasure, an unfairness, even the possibility of anarchy remains in your pocket for life.

When the film *If...* came out in 1968 in England, all those boys who had gone to English public schools found the release of revenge. Up to that moment there had been nothing to represent their fury at those marbled principles they had tunnelled into and that had ruined or deformed them in some way. It was how we too had burrowed through the junior boarding school at Winchester House with those same rules that Skanda must have witnessed earlier, that always gave him his grim grin of remembrance. He would be courteous, socially wise as an adult, even while remembering the boys playing cricket—all of them so young and forever anonymous in that picture, without seeming to have a care in the world. But he knew as we did that the dragon who governed the boarding school was a Father Barnabas, and no one who survived that time would ever forget his name, or forgive him a half century later.

He had come disguised into our childhood world wearing the dark cassock of a priest, his large body belted with a Christian cord of rope. He probably thrashed every boy numerous times in the two or three years they would be under his academic and supposed spiritual care, until they escaped and moved eventually into mid-school, boarding later at Copleston House, where the dormitories felt safer even if Dickensian in their rules. Those were the years when we learned to protect ourselves by becoming liars, being devious, never confessing to a crime, in fact confessing to nothing, good or bad. Such as pouring petrol and setting fire to the rhododendron bush in the small garden belonging to Father Barnabas—right beside his window as if the light from it could witness his crimes. In any case, a group of us would continue to meet at the "fives court," cut open our palms with a razor blade, in order to be on the side of the devil, swearing an eight-year-old's blood oath against that black-cassocked body for the rest of our lives, until he would die painfully, perhaps strangled by one of us with that Christian cord, or until another flowering bush caught fire during the night.

Skanda had given me—it now appears—an ironic remembrance of boys playing cricket without a care in the world, where an hour of sport was all. As if violence could belong only to the climate, brief as a rain shower. But during those years we were really being taught to fear the future. If priests were like this, what would prefects be like? Or roughs we might meet in the real world, clutching only the sweetness and safety of a black-and-white photograph?

There would be other photographs that recorded other schools I went to, in another country, with their varying methods of law and judgement. Those future places were more innocent, less dangerous. None of them would have known of a man named Barnabas, or the way some of us still tracked his career to discover where he might be living in the last years of his life, with a small dog in a one-room apartment on South Bridge Road in Singapore, where he could be visited by a former student who, having located his address, partially strangled him with the rope and then cut his throat with a rusty knife so he fell back over a kitchen table and expired there.

But nothing of the truth of Father Barnabas would be revealed. Only now and then, for a few years afterwards, his name would appear in letters written back and forth between a group of us, or appear in the fictional world of Cassius in *The Cat's Table*, who especially loathed him for the habitual beatings that still returned as a poisonous dream. And when the film *If...* years later depicted an imaginary revolution in an English school it meant little to those in a far country. It was shown briefly at the Savoy in Wellawatte on the Galle Road, but by then Father Barnabas had left the scene of the crime.

Lakdhas Wikkramasinha, one of the best poets in Sri Lanka, claimed he always wrote in an "immoralist style." He had gone to that school. Later he studied law, and wrote remarkable poems, argumentative, political, hating the school he had been sent to, speaking often of terrible events on that campus. Apart from his own poetry, he translated poems from eighteenth-century Sinhala as well as poets from abroad whom he loved and admired, like García Lorca and Mandelstam. Before he married, he had said to his wife, "I will have to get rid of all of these feelings of fear and insecurity that have been second nature to me." Although in the end, Lakdhas would have a brief life. In 1978, at the age of thirty-six he would drown in the sea off Mount Lavinia close to our school, as if still caught in its tides and currents.

But the impetus for a magical *If*-like revolution for those who went to that school in Colombo could have been provided by Lakdhas in a poem he wrote called "1950–1959."

Under the nightmare of Saint Thomas he wandered

. . . in the quadrangle he mocked himself to sleep
how could he say "my brother" to the scum who ruled the day

beaten with their sticks what lament formed in his mind
ruined the heart . . .

in the haze of pain, under the hoarse breath of enemies
drunken masters beat him to the wall

Even now the poem evokes the landscape of that school faultlessly, where everything described felt damaged— "the broken-willed trees"—and where every phrase—the hoarse breath of enemies, the stigmatic spirit, the cold beds, the drunken masters—depicts danger. It is the poem one would wish to have cut into stone on the grounds of that school, written in that voice of "fear and insecurity" which had become second nature to him. All of that needs to be remembered, or there would be no warning of what had existed there. Today the junior boarding school of Winchester House no longer exists. His poem is the memorial it deserves.

*

There is one more moment to complete that abandoned time. Stories, letters, films, memoirs of our youth, are nothing without some real clue or glance towards the truth. Otherwise in the past there is only a bale of hay we pause at with no understanding and with no recognition of an evil. There was no midnight strangling with a rope, no rusty blade to cut his throat—as we might have wished to tell it. Except as Lakdhas does in his poem—"How could he say 'my brother' to the scum who ruled the day."

Many years later, returning to Sri Lanka, I got to know the archaeologist Senake Bandaranayake about the same time that I began to discover the poems of Lakdhas Wikkramasinha and just as I met Skanda again. We had all been sent to Winchester House, and the place had become for us the eye of a needle each of us had crawled through.

Senake and I became very close friends. And we talked often of the dragon in his black robe. Then he told me a story. Being a well-known archaeologist, Senake had been invited to Singapore to give a series of lectures. A few days before returning to Colombo he received a phone call at his Singapore hotel from Father Barnabas who had read of his visit in the newspapers. Barnabas was now very old. His wife had died years before, and he was living in an apartment in a nearby area. He invited Senake to stay with him, perhaps on his last night? So they could catch up? After all, they were both from Sri Lanka. . . .

Senake hesitated. He had disliked those years at St. Thomas, specifically being boarded at Winchester House. He had been beaten like the rest of us. He recalled those years as far more demonic, for instance, than the world of *Tom Brown's School Days*. But for whatever reason, maybe wishing for some kind of understanding, he arrived late in the evening after his talk, met the old teacher who lived there alone with his small dog, and they talked quite late into the night. And then Senake slept on the sofa until, in the middle of the night, he awakened to crying. The old man weeping. Senake got up, walked into Barnabas's bedroom and saw the old priest beating the dog.

"THERE ARE THREE SOUNDS IN THE WOOD THIS MORNING"

writes Edward Thomas.
Each day he walks the fields in his journal
beside that narrow river, a one-word hill,
with a pause of space he leaves for any bird call

He is the sentinel of quiet places
where nothing supposedly happens,
as when he arrived at Adlestrop by train
and found nothing there, until he listened longer

"Still not a thrush—but many blackbirds,"
he would write, in his last letter,
near the battlefield in Arras in 1917,
those few days before he died

At certain seasons rivers follow literature.
A stream enters the Edo Gardens north of Kyoto,
trespasses under the Plum-Gate, and wanders
by the tower designed by Ishikawa Jōzan,
where his few guests whistled at the moon.

In the Thames estuary hours from Dover, the brackish waters
familiar to readers of Dickens—the River Crouch, Ship Wash,
West Sunk, Foulness Sands, the Feather Channel—hide
unspoken adventures. Southeast is still the River Medway
where Magwitch escaped his prison ship, lowering himself
with the tide into a Kent marsh, to begin his story
the way someone might emerge tonight restless
out of another river.

Rivers remember voices, someone's name, a guilt.

So Ishikawa Jōzan disguised portraits of his lovers
with a concave-convex style before their eventual farewells.
                              Few clues remained of them.
"So many thunderstorms," one wrote him later in
a season of storms, "with no damage as elsewhere
—just the thrill. And birdsong distinct, as if these
were your lines in a memoir."

They would all leave Shisendō for lives in distant villages.
Who remembers them or those journeys now? Not even me.

For years I knew where friends and heroines abided
until they followed the light of another career.
"I married / in the world's black night / for warmth /
if not repose."

Forgotten journeys reveal themselves now
like silence, the way waterfalls, surveyed years ago
on the Cataraqui River east of the Perth Road,
"that should have been exploding still," are no longer heard.

So the past becomes an undiscovered country.
Only in classics are there reliable maps of searching or desire—
"He was a league from Verrières, on the road to Geneva.
'If there is any suspicion,' thought Julien,
'it's on the Paris road that they will look for me.'"
Or in his unconfessed passion in an unlit room,
where the lovers had not even seen each other,
so complete was the darkness.
"You must soon leave me," she whispered in a curt tone,
their hungry romance articulated in an earlier chapter.
(She had found it impossible to "purloin" any bread.)

Other lives ignored the distances of travel. Stanley Spencer
witnessed the universe in Cookham, including the dead.
Arthur Waley, at 50 Gordon Square near the British Museum,
translated Chinese poetry, Mongol history, *The Tale of Genji*
—never journeying more than a few miles from London,
and buried in an unmarked grave, Plot 51178, in Highgate Cemetery.

As Keeper of Oriental Prints he knew "somewhere, someone
is always traveling furiously toward you," on a distant rail

or alongside desert tribes speaking other languages
with their knowledge of great rivers, estuaries.

Years later the thief and murderer entered London
in coarse grey, crossing Blackfriars Bridge, the scar
from an iron shackle still on his leg. He was sixty years old.
He had journeyed along Upper Maidenhead Road, sleeping
in graveyards, gathering the thrown-out bread from bakeries
as he entered the city.
                    Meanwhile there was a crisis in his writer's life.
Dickens also was walking the city at night, holding onto a romance
Nelly Ternan Nelly Ternan Nelly Ternan entering
a train station to watch the morning mail come in.
Only in daylight could he find sleep.

                              *

There are traditions of night discoveries even without a jour-
ney. Artists find rooms that do not contain electricity and
work without light, no longer confident of the closeness of
the new paint against the already drawn eye. Just as leaning
over a long breath of prose will allow you a longer less certain
walk to clarify your half-formed thoughts about one now lost
to you. It was the way desert explorers altered maps during
dreams when tiredness allowed them "aimless thoughts to
strike themselves alight" so they might find that simpler, less
complex route to Basra, where nothing until then seemed to
exist.

It was always a guess, a leap. The way Ezra Pound allowed
Li Po to reach Kensington by way of Tokyo, or how a sea-
captain used his old hand-drawn map instead of nautical

charts to let him escape into a book called *Victory*. Perhaps it was even the way the whole landscape and plot of a great literary war came to life because of "a thought that was called Helen."

There's undefended sleeplessness in writing, like those shifting estuaries that take place during a game of Go. "You wake, quickly throw words down," says Tomas Tranströmer, "but in the morning the words don't say anything anymore, are scrawls or fragments of a great mighty style that dragged past." Or sometimes names and words appear only in code.

There are places where language refuses to meet a reader, like cursive scripts that flow as if unawakened, or those lost voices of waterfalls. It can occur even where you attempt to end your story—some improbable place, as a friend once wrote, that you will walk through only after you are dead, your bare feet on an ancient mosaic in Tunis that could perhaps guide you like a terza rima towards a safe place to complete your story.

Lafcadio Hearn claimed that in ancient Japanese texts there are numerous explanations "curiously preserved" for why fiction or poetry is left unfinished. Perhaps the writer was called away from his small table and never returned. Or death might stop his writing brush in the middle of a sentence. Perhaps there was a sudden lack of certainty caused by the disappearance of a fictional character in a sleepless book someone was writing—so now there was no longer a tender convict or friend the author had discovered hiding somewhere in his or her youth.

During those eras and landscapes of a writer's life, alongside the black horizontal marshes of Essex or in that Edo residence of a Japanese recluse whose portraits could be discerned only by "the flying white" in his calligraphy, there were times when a character or even their story could be lost. We might forget our destination and have to recall how to get there by following a person we had invented. Despite his sudden departure and ending, I would remember Ramadhin and, even earlier, the woman Alice Gull, who lived only within their fictional worlds. As if somehow there could be during their invention, in Zbigniew Herbert's phrase, "the blessed invisibility of a life."

"The thing with Madonnas," I had written, "is they have that look on their faces. They can see the finished map. They know He is going to die when young. And this was the look, the long-distance gaze towards her son with his unsafe heart I would see on Ramadhin's mother's face." Or within that other story, fearful already of her future, I once had whispered to myself in a paragraph, "Let me stay in this field with Alice Gull." As if they were like brief lives I had grown up with and then lost over the years.

In Highgate Cemetery you find in unmarked graves their unfinished thoughts, anonymous as explorers who came along unnamed rivers or as a convict calculating at dawn the speed of the lowering tide, and learning the name and speech of a boy through whom he might enter a human world. He too now crawls nameless into an unmarked grave. What a noise their lives once made!

Though what will remain is this surprising pleasure of silence that Zbigniew Herbert claims for Piero della Francesca whose life is now so hidden by his paintings it is impossible to place him in any story. "He has received the greatest act of mercy by absent-minded history, which mislays documents and blurs all traces of life." His grave is similar to the quiet grave of my childhood companion Rosalin Perera, now on a distant hill as she will always exist for me, a person who had once gone ahead, whom now I see behind. In that blessed invisibility of a life where "all were kind, all were strangers."

For years we have talked like this in a river
after months away, how we missed each other,
what we discovered or argued over when apart.
Our stories stitched together the lost winter,
and what occurred in February when this river froze
having been abandoned by us.

We are in this usual gathering place, telling stories
that always begin a certain way, recalling a possibly
altered life, as if within the wide liberty of a novel
—where you might trespass into a field during a first chapter,
or board a crowded train and claim this is where you fell in love.
It is how a person might reveal a desire among friends with no
    foothold
in this river, only a cloud's reflection holding you up.

Each afternoon the four or five of us break into song.
Chuck Berry's "Memphis, Tennessee," Zevon's "A Certain Girl,"
remembered from an earlier time when none of us knew each
    other,
when that storm of music had not yet arrived.

Now we are with each other's children
where there might be a sudden embrace
over a sadness, someone's loss.

But on certain nights the river will rise because
of a released or altered lock a mile north of here
and the canoe that rests on rock will rise
with the water and float away, untethered.

You go after it. You swim downstream with a paddle
to reach it, steer it back.

You journey beyond the familiar properties, find yourself
before long in anonymous water, nothing audible from shore,
only the shake of reflection like a breaking word.
Is this a different mood of the Black River?
With daylight there is the disguised location of the stars.
You recall other journeys where you crisscrossed Lanark
or Frontenac County from river to river and entered
the scuttle holes of the Moira, to swim its maze
of underwater rock you shall never find again.
There were so many streams with abandoned names,
their riverbeds wordless. Whereas elsewhere
rivers even described themselves—the wide Missouri,
the Qu'Appelle, "who calls?"

You swim into late afternoon. The past more distant,
more alive. One late spring you sensed your way east,
portaging over fields as if through a post-war landscape.
You forget that river's name you came to, where you beached
the borrowed canoe, entered a café and danced with her for an
    hour
beside a juke box, faithless near that small river whose creeks had
merged, disguising themselves within another river's name.

He remembers her there by that nameless river, long after,
still envious of himself at that time.

All those echoing rivers where we lost or found ourselves.
Who calls? Who calls?
There was the girl by the Clare River, he remembers now
as he swims into evening with the arrival of those stars.

ACKNOWLEDGEMENTS

Thank you to the writers whose works I have quoted at various moments in this book. A line from a poem by Grace Paley and a line from Thomas Merton both appear in "A Night Radio Station in Koprivshtitsa." A waking thought from Tomas Tranströmer's *Baltics* appears in the poem "Estuaries." Cole Swensen and James Salter are quoted in "Wanderer," as is Linda Gregg in "A Bus to Fez," and Lorine Niedecker in "Estuaries." The painting, from the Ross-Coomaraswamy Collection in the Museum of Fine Arts Boston, *Woman Swinging from a Mango Tree*, is the source of the poem "A Disappearance." A stanza from Paul Vermeersch's poem "Lost Things" appears in "Bruise." Eric Folsom and Steven Heighton, both river poets, have written about the lost sound of old waterfalls. There is a couplet by Agha Shahid Ali in "Last Things." Lines from a last letter by the poet Edward Thomas to his wife appear in "There are three sounds in the wood this morning," and a sentence from his poem "Over the Hills" ends "Estuaries." Zbigniew Herbert's comments about Piero della Francesca appear in his *Collected Prose*. I would also like to acknowledge Ariane Mnouchkine and Le Théâtre du Soleil for their wondrous film *Molière*, as well as the sometimes seemingly anonymous Chris Marker for that brief and classic film *La Jetée*, which led to writing "Into the Past."

Thank you to Shanthini Gunawardhana, Senake Bandaranayake, Aparna Halpé, Howard Norman, and Gregor von Rezzori, as well as Little Toller Books in Dorset.

Memories sometimes grow during the remembering of them. My portrait of the character Skanda in "Winchester House" is a combination of invention, unreliable memory, and his already fictional appearance as a doctor in *Anil's Ghost*. As some readers might notice I have occasionally enlarged or rewritten scenes from earlier work. Nothing remains still in a story.

*

Many thanks to McClelland & Stewart in Canada and Alfred A. Knopf in the USA, and to my great editors, Louise Dennys and Daniel Halpern; as well as all those involved with the design and production of this book—especially the remarkable Katherine Hourigan, who has choreographed and guided all my books through Knopf since 1991; and to Rob Shapiro, Kimberlee Kemp, Pei Loi Koay, Lorraine Hyland, Kevin Bourke, John Gall, Kim Kandravy, and Andrea Synowicki; as well as to Ashley Dunn and Josephine Kals. Thanks also to Stephanie Sinclair in Toronto and to Jordan Pavlin in New York for their unwavering support.

As always, appreciation and love to my dear allies—Ellen Levine, Steven Barclay, and Tulin Valeri.

Thanks also to friends who shared rivers with us for over forty years—including Bob Carney, Lora Senechal, Robbie Fyfe, Nancy Beatty, and Stan Dragland.

And to the great musician Ben Webster who, when told he could have three wishes, remarked, "Right now, I wish I could write a couple of tunes."

TEXT PERMISSIONS

From *The Narrow Road to the Deep North and Other Travel Sketches* by Matsuo Bashō published by Penguin Classics. Copyright © Nobuyuki Yuasa, 1966. Reprinted by permission of Penguin Books Limited.

Linda Gregg, excerpt from "Forget All That" from *Too Bright to See / Alma*. Copyright © 1985 by Linda Gregg. Reprinted with the permission of The Permissions Company, LLC, on behalf of Graywolf Press, graywolfpress.org.

Seven lines from Lakdhas Wikkramasinha's poem "1950–1959," courtesy of *New York Review of Books* and the Lakdhas Wikkramasinha estate.

A NOTE ABOUT THE AUTHOR

MICHAEL ONDAATJE is the author of seven novels, a memoir, *Running in the Family*; a nonfiction book on cinema, *The Conversations: Walter Murch and the Art of Editing Film*; and several books of poetry, including *The Cinnamon Peeler* and *Handwriting*. *The English Patient* received the Booker Prize in 1992 and the Golden Man Booker in 2018, and was made into a film directed by Anthony Minghella; *Anil's Ghost* was awarded the Irish Times International Fiction Prize, the Giller Prize, and the Prix Médicis. Born in Sri Lanka, Michael Ondaatje lives in Toronto.

A NOTE ON THE TYPE

This book was set in Jenson, a font designed for the Adobe
Corporation by Robert Slimbach in 1995. Jenson is an inter-
pretation of the famous Venetian type cut in 1469 by the
Frenchman Nicolas Jenson (c. 1420–1480).

Composed by North Market Street Graphics,
Lancaster, Pennsylvania

Printed and bound by Friesens,
Altona, Manitoba

Book design by Pei Loi Koay